Do Not Quit, Viv!

By Carmel Reilly

It is a fun run for kids!

Viv and Quin can run.

Quin has a big red wig.

Viv has a cat hat
and cat top.

Quin runs.

He is fit.

Quin jets up to the top.

Viv runs.

But Viv is hot.

She quits!

Viv has a sip and gets up.

Viv jogs a lap!

Quin did not win.

But Quin and Viv
got to the top!

CHECKING FOR MEANING

1. What did Viv wear at the fun run? *(Literal)*

2. Why did Viv quit? *(Literal)*

3. Why didn't Quin win the fun run? *(Inferential)*

EXTENDING VOCABULARY

quit	Look at the word *quit*. What letter follows the *q* in this word? What do you notice about the other words that start with *q* in the book?
jets	What is the meaning of the word *jets* in the book? What else can it mean?
fun run	The words *fun* and *run* rhyme. What other words can you think of that rhyme with *fun* and *run*?

MOVING BEYOND THE TEXT

1. Why do you think the children in the fun run were dressed up?

2. Would you like to be in a fun run? Why or why not?

3. What do you think Quin might do to keep fit?

4. Is winning always important? Why or why not?

SPEED SOUNDS

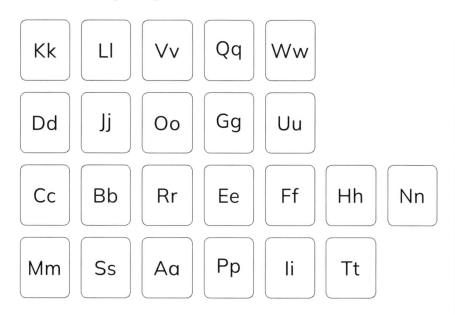

Kk Ll Vv Qq Ww

Dd Jj Oo Gg Uu

Cc Bb Rr Ee Ff Hh Nn

Mm Ss Aa Pp Ii Tt

PRACTICE WORDS

Viv

Quin

wig

quit

win

lap

kids

quits

lots

laps